I0161472

Labour Law

J.K. Kelei, LL.M

SSP

Gak Law Firm Edition
GLF 1st Edition © 2020

Author: J.K. Kelei, LL.M

Bor Publishers © 2020 – Australia, Perth.

First published by Bor Publishers – Australia.

Legal & Disclaimer

The information contained in this book and its contents is not designed to replace or take the place of any form of professional advice; and is not meant to replace the need for independent, legal or other professional advice or services, as may be required. The content and information in this book has been provided for educational and entertainment purposes only.

The content and information contained in this book has been compiled from sources deemed reliable, and it is accurate to the best of the Author's knowledge, information and belief. However, the Author cannot guarantee its accuracy and validity and cannot be held liable for any errors and/or omissions. Further, changes are periodically made to this book as and when needed. Where appropriate and/or necessary, you must consult a professional (including but not limited to your attorney or other professional advisor) before using any of the suggested information in this book.

Bor Publishers,
Perth, Western Australia

Phone: 08 9439 4704

ABN: 45 867 024 044

ISBN: 978-0-6482848-8-8

BP

Bor Publishers

www.borpublishers.com
admin@borpublishers.com

DEDICATION

This book is dedicated to South Sudan's unions, employers and employees to serve better employability and promote safe working environment for all.

CONTENTS

ACRONYM

ILO	International Labour Organisation
CRC	Convention on the Rights of the Child
AU	African Union
UK	United Kingdom
ERA	Employment Rights Act 1996 of UK
EAT	Employment Appeal Tribunal of UK
UN	United Nations
IGAD	Intergovernmental Authority on Development
EU	European Union

ACKNOWLEDGMENTS

I would like to thank all people who gave me their supports in printing of this Book.

FOREWORD

Labour law came to be a force to reckon with during the Industrial Revolution era. Since the transition or surge from small-scale production to large-scale factory, it was imperative that the relationship between employer and employees changed. Working under extreme conditions and unsafe environment prompted workers to seek for the right to join labour union. Most times, the stats of labour law is usually the product of as well as an element of forces between several social forces.

Labour law in most part of the world creates an assurance between the three bodies involved i.e., the employer, employee, and union. Traditionally, the least socially acceptable situations where contractors or mostly employees are permitted to work is referred to as employment standards. Usually this is enforced by the government i.e. the judicial or legislative.

Going by the first country to industrialize, England was also the first to experience the damning consequences of the industrial revolution from workers strikes in a much less regulated economic system. This went on for long particularly in the 18th century to the early-mid 19th century, slowly but carefully the foundation for modern labour law was established. More importantly, the appalling aspects of working conditions were progressively improved through legislation.

The major principle that runs through most labour law is the liberty of both parties to draw out individual contracting. Being that the

1

relationship between employer and employee is very much voluntary and both parties enter into agreements formulated by themselves with the constraints obligated by the law of contract. Although the law of contract allows equal freedom, it is not outright with the inequality innate in the relationship between employee and employer.

Asides, fighting against the appalling working conditions, injustice a worker may experience, and many more. Trade unions (promotes the interests of its members) acting as a bridge between employee and employer. The republic of South Sudan's labour law is to create a legal framework for the barest conditions of employment, labour institutions, dispute resolution, health and safety institutions in accordance with the constitution as well as in conformity with the regional and international onuses of South Sudan.

Majok Wutchok |MPH|GDPH|Bsc-Hons Nutrition|

Chief Operating Officer |Bor Publishers |Maked Technology|

Principal Web Developer| Publisher| Author | Researcher |Blogger|

Business Websites|www.borpublishers.com|www.makedtech.com|

Blog Sites | www.jubahealth.com | www.mentalhelper.com |

CHAPTER ONE

Introduction of Labour Law in General

There is something fundamental to a person's identity about work. "People's jobs are their lives,"[1]

Labour law has traditionally encompassed the relationships among unions, employers, and employees. Labour laws grant employees in labour market the right to unionize and allow employers and employees to engage in certain workplace-related activities (for example, strikes and lockouts) in order to further their demands for changes in the employer-employee relationship.

Employment law, on the other hand, is defined more broadly as the negotiated relationships between employers and employees. Although employment lawyers deal with many of the same parties as labour lawyers (i.e., workers and companies), they conventionally address issues that fall outside the framework of union-management relations and collective bargaining. As a result, the extent to which statutes or regulations pertain to unions and union-workers usually determines whether or not they are regarded as components of "labour law" or "employment law."

Given the distinguishable set of issues encompassed in each field, labour law and employment law remain discrete areas of practice. However, these two fields have, over time, become increasingly symbiotic. Careers in either field can involve both labour and employment law questions. This book will give you a better sense of understanding of the major principle of labour law,

---

[1] Kyle Edwards et al, Labour and Employment Law: A Career Guide, 2012.

so that you are better able to comprehend the labour market.

The labour market is constantly evolving. Since workplaces often change faster than the laws that govern them, attorneys must regularly rethink how this field should look in the present and in the future. The law relating to labour in South Sudan deals mainly with the regulation of the contract of employment under which the employee undertakes to work for his employer, for financial reward.

The main doctrine, which runs through the labour law, is that the parties are free to make their own contracts. The relationship between employer and employee is a voluntary relationship into which the parties may enter on terms laid down by themselves within the limitations imposed by the law of contract. The law of contract, however, assumes that there is equal freedom in the parties to enter into a contract, however it is silence about the inequality inherent in the employment relationship.[2] It ignores the superior economic strength and the bargaining power of the employer *vis-a-vis* the person who has to make a living getting employment, or perhaps starves.[3] In order to redress the imbalance in employment sphere, the employees through their numbers, have sought to organize themselves into trade union and adopt the method of collective bargaining. From this standpoint, they also sought legislative protection and privileges by exercising their political influence. This resulted into intervention of the States to effectively protect the workers by regulating matters like safety, health and welfare, hours of work, leave and holidays and social security.

---

[2] Anand Prakash and Revised by Dr. S S. Jaswal, Labour Law.
[3] Ibid.

In South Sudan, legislation relating to labour has just started mainly after the enactment of the Labour Act, 2017. Till 2017, South Sudan was using Sudanese legislation to regulate the field. One may, broadly, stated that labour law of South Sudan is based on the doctrine of laissez-faire also known as freedom of contract, and it thus recognized the need for adequate legal protection to labour market participants. Labour legislation in South Sudan should now become a basis for social and economic legislation, which derived its inspiration and recognition of the wider social-economic responsibilities, which the state must undertake to protect the and socially and economically weaker sections of the society. These are often summed up under the convenient heading of the 'welfare state', whose responsibility it is to assure to its citizens not only physical liberty to pursue their avocations according to their liking, and political liberty to choose their own government at reasonable intervals, but also assure social well-being and economic opportunities to make the foregoing liberties meaningful and effective.[4]

For clarity purpose, we will divide the subject into five topics. One may warn that It will be wrong, to think that those topics are not related. As a matter of fact, they overlap, and the division into various topics is to help the learners to understand the main features of labour law. Contract of employment will be handle under chapter two. Termination of contract of employment will be discussed under chapter three. Issues to do with health, welfare, working conditions and hours of work including leave and holidays will be handled under chapter four, while vicarious liability will be dealt with under chapter five. At last but not least, labour unions will be handled under chapter six.

---

[4] Ibid.

I.I The Scope of the Field

Before one could proceeds to the main topics of this book, one would want to first highlight the relation between Labour and Employment Law.

Labour law basically encompassed the relationships among unions, employers and employees. Labour laws gives employees in labour market the right to organize themselves into unions and allow employers and employees to participate in workplace-related activities e.g. strikes and lockouts, in order to further their demands for changes in the employer-employee relationship. On the other hand, employment law covers broadly issues of the negotiated relationships between employers and employees. Although employment legal expertise deals with the same parties as labour legal expertise i.e., workers and companies, they conventionally address issues that fall outside the framework of union-management relations and collective bargaining.[5] As a result, the extent to which statutes or regulations pertain to unions and union-workers usually determines whether or not they are regarded as components of "labour law" or "employment law."[6]

Based on the above distinguishable set of matters contained in each field, labour law and employment law remain discrete disciplines of law. Nevertheless, these two fields have, over time, become increasingly interdependent. Issues of labour market in either field can involve both labour and employment law questions.

However, the vagueness of the terms "labour and employment law" can deter law students and advocates when considered alongside easily definable fields, such as environmental law, administrative law, or banking law.

---

[5] Kyle Edwards et al, Labour and Employment Law: A Career Guide, 2012
[6] Ibid.

Nonetheless labour and employment law is truly adaptable field that oftentimes touches on issues that arise in a wide range of other legal disciplines.

Labour legal experts primarily work in or on behalf of unions and their members. The work of labour lawyers range from negotiating collective bargaining agreements on behalf of union members to advising union leaders, to representing individual union members in arbitration proceedings. While, on the other hand, union-management relations are governed by Labour Act, 2017 and their Internal Rules and Regulations. Workers' demand for collective action usually force open alternative legal channels, which include collective campaigns in which workers turn to Labour Act, 2017, as the legal base that facilitates and protects their collective activities. As unions and their members participate in so many different industries and activities, labour lawyers normally face legal issues that fall outside the realm of the traditional labour statutes.

Employment legal experts encounter a variety of issues related to the governance and structure of employment relationships in a non-union sphere. To mention but a few, those are issues including wage and working hours, discrimination, workplace health and safety, pensions and benefits, and workers' compensation in case of injuries. In addition, employment lawyers may also deal with issues that are typically considered to be part of labour law e.g. (the ability of workers to enforce employment rights collectively.

I.II General Principles of Labour Law

Internationally, the International Labour Organization (ILO) is the United Nations agency that was established United Nations General

Assembly for the purpose of setting international labour standards. The ILO is structured in a tripartite structure, which comprises government's representatives, employers and employees' representatives.

Labour principles derive from ILO Conventions and Recommendations, which set international labour standards on a broad range of subjects related to the world of work, including human rights at work, occupational safety and health, employment policy and human resources development. Increasing concerns about the social impact of globalization led the members of the ILO - representatives of government, employers and workers at the international level - to recognize in 1995 that there were four categories of labour principles and rights, expressed in eight conventions (the so-called "core conventions"), that should be considered as fundamental because they protect basic workers' rights.[7]

These categories are:

a. Freedom of association and the effective recognition of the right to collective bargaining;

b. The elimination of all forms of forced or compulsory labour;

c. The effective abolition of child labour; and

d. The elimination of discrimination in respect of employment and occupation.

It is a must know for the students of law and legal experts of Labour Law of the following core Labour Conventions and they are:

a. Freedom of Association and Protection of the Right to Organize Convention (No. 87), 1948, and

b. Right to Organize and Collective Bargaining Convention (No. 98), 1949.

---

[7] The Labour Principles of the United Nations Global Compact: A Guide for Business / International Labour Office. - Geneva: ILO, 2008, Page 9.

Those are the Conventions providing legal basis on promotion of freedom of association and right to collective bargaining.

    c.   Forced Labour Convention (No. 29), 1930, and

    d.   Abolition of Forced Labour Convention (No. 105), 1957.

Those are the Conventions providing legal basis on prohibition of forced labour.

    e.   Minimum Age Convention (No. 138), 1973, and

    f.   Worst Form of Child Labour Convention (No. 182), 1999.

Those are the Conventions providing legal basis on prohibition of child labour.

    g.   Equal Remuneration Convention (No. 100), 1951, and

    h.   Discrimination (Employment and Occupation) Convention (No. 111), 1958.

Those are the Conventions providing legal basis on prohibition of employment and occupation discrimination.

a. *Important of the Principle of Freedom of Association and Collective Bargaining*

The principles of freedom of association infers to a respect for the right of all employers and employees to freely and voluntarily establish and join unions for the promotion and defence of their occupational interests. It also implies that employees and employers have the right to set up, join and run their own unions without interference from the State or any another entity.

Furthermore, it means that employers should not interfere in employees' decision to associate, or try to influence their decision by any mean, or discriminate against either those employees who choose to associate or those who represent them.

The right of employees, on the other hand, to bargain freely with employers is an important component in freedom of association. In according to ILO, *"collective bargaining is a voluntary process through which employers and workers discuss and negotiate their relations, in particular terms and conditions of work"*.

Collective bargaining can function best if all parties conduct it freely and in good faith. This means:

a. Willingness and an efforts to reach an agreement;

b. Negotiate constructively and genuinely;

c. Avoid unjustified delays;

d. Honouring and applying the collective agreements concluded in good faith; and

e. Readiness to give sufficient time for the parties to amicably settle disputes.

The aim of bargaining in good faith is to reach mutually acceptable collective agreements. In case there is no agreement reached, dispute settlement procedures e.g. conciliation through mediation to arbitration may be used.

In order to realise the principle of freedom of association and the right to collective bargaining requires a legal basis, which safeguards the enforcement of such rights. Enforcement also requires an enabling institutional framework, which is tripartite, between the labour enforcement agency, employers' and employees' organizations, or combinations of both.

Employees who, individually, wish to exercise their right to have their voice heard must be also protected from discrimination. For the sake of mutual benefit, employers' and employees' organizations are expected to accept each other as partners in order to be able to solve joint problems and deals with mutual challenges.

For the above, governments have the responsibility to ensure that the legal and institutional frameworks do exist and functional. The government should also help to promote a culture of mutual acceptance and cooperation, while enforcing the principle of freedom of association and collective bargaining.

In addition to being a right, "freedom of association enables workers and employers to join together to protect better not only their own economic interests but also their civil freedoms such as the right to life, security, integrity, and personal and collective freedom. As an integral part of democracy, this principle is crucial in order to realize all other fundamental principles and rights at work".[8]

b. *Important of the Principle of the elimination of all forms of forced and compulsory labour*

Forced or compulsory labour is any work or service that a person has not offered him-/herself voluntarily to do or any work that is exacted from any person under threat of penalty. It has to be made clear that provision of wages or other compensation to an employee does not necessarily mean that the labour is not forced or compulsory. Legally, labour should be freely given and employees should be free to leave, subject to adequate notice within

---

[8] The Labour Principles of the United Nations Global Compact: A Guide for Business / International Labour Office. - Geneva: ILO, 2008, Page 18.

reasonable time.

The ILO estimates that "at least 12.3 million people are victims of forced labour worldwide, 80 per cent of which is exacted by private agents. Most victims receive little or no earnings, and work for long hours in extremely poor conditions of health and safety".[9]

The exploitation in labour market may occur in different forms, however, forced labour is something different. It occurs where labour is exacted by the State or individuals who have the power to threaten employees with sanctions, such as denial of food, land or wages and use of physical violence or sexual abuse, or restricting peoples' movements and it sometimes can go as far as detention of the people. Companies can be involves in practice of forced labour through their business associates.

c. *Important of the prohibition of Child Labour*

Conventions establishing minimum age Convention and the worst forms of child labour provides the legal framework for national authorities to prescribe a minimum age for employment of children who are still at the age of compulsory schooling, and in any case not less than fourteen (14) years.

Tab. 1

ILO Convention Minimum Age for Admission to Employment[10]		
	Developed Countries	Developing Countries
Regular Work	15 years	14 years

---

[9] The Labour Principles of the United Nations Global Compact: A Guide for Business / International Labour Office. - Geneva: ILO, 2008, Page 21.
[10] Minimum Age Convention (No. 138), 1973.

Hazardous Work	18 years	18 years
Light work	13 years	12 years

Child labour should not be confused with "youth employment"; as from the minimum working age, young people should be able to engage in decent work, but still need protection from hazardous work and other worst forms of child labour.[11]

It is therefore compulsory that companies should make efforts to eliminate all forms of child labour and in so doing, efforts to eliminate the worst forms of child labour must not be used to justify other forms of child labour. Reason being: child labour damage child's physical, social and psychological development. "Child labour deprives children of their childhood and their dignity".[12]

d. Important of prohibition of discrimination in employment and occupation

Discrimination in employment and occupation can occurs when a candidate is treated differently or less favourably because of his/her race, colour, sex, religion, political alignment, or social origin.[13] This can clearly be seen in access to employment, or particular occupations, training and social security. Moreover, it can occur with respect to the terms and conditions of employment, such as:[14]

- Recruitment;

- Remuneration;

---

[11] The Labour Principles of the United Nations Global Compact: A Guide for Business / International Labour Office. - Geneva: ILO, 2008, Page 27.
[12] Ibid.
[13] Labour Act, 2017, section 6(3).
[14] The Labour Principles of the United Nations Global Compact: A Guide for Business / International Labour Office. - Geneva: ILO, 2008, Page 27.

- Hours of work and rest, paid holidays;
- Maternity protection;
- Security of tenure;
- Job assignments;
- Performance assessment and advancement;
- Training opportunities;
- Promotion prospects;
- Occupational safety and health; and
- Termination of employment.

The question that pose itself hereafter is: what is non-discriminative labour practice? The answer is simple. Non-discrimination is when employees are employed on the basis of their merit and professionalism to do the job without favouritism, or preference made on race, colour, sex, religion, political alignment, or social origin. Labour discrimination affects the individual concerned and negatively influences his/her contribution to society.

A company that practices labour discrimination denies itself access to talents from a wider pool of skills and competencies. In addition, the pain and resentment generated by such practices affect the performance of individuals and teams in the company. "Discriminatory practices result in missed opportunities for development of skills and infrastructure to strengthen competitiveness in the national and global economy".[15] Last but not the least, discrimination can harm a company's status, and thus potentially affect profits and stock value.

---

[15] The Labour Principles of the United Nations Global Compact: A Guide for Business / International Labour Office. - Geneva: ILO, 2008, Page 33.

I.III Labour Law in Brief

Throughout the early age, working conditions for the average worker were and still are grim. We can also see the used of child labour and discrimination of all types are common and acceptable. There is also a high prevalence of negligent of safety regulations of hazardous working conditions are order of the day. Inexperience of employees unions made bargaining for better conditions very difficult for workers. There is therefore a need in few years for active unions and government institutions in order to make a number of changes to make life for the South Sudanese workers more tolerable. The convergence of a variety of social and legal shifts can create the environment necessary for such change.

a. *Evolution of the nation met by an evolution of the law*

As international community of which South Sudan is a part, has placed more value on education and child welfare, child protection laws have ensured that more children take advantage of education and the freedom currently associated with childhood.

As a consequent of a rigours child rights advocacy and globalisation, South Sudanese societies become less concerned with traditional gender roles. The legal regime promoting equality between men and women have increased the opportunities for women in the labour market. Though still seen very conservative, South Sudanese developed tolerant of both women and minority rights.

Many people has become more concern about the safety of workers, a concern which should leads to enactment of laws that will contribute to a decline in the number of workers lost to grievous workplace injuries, e.g. in petroleum and mining sector.

With the beginning of national labour laws, which are aimed at protections for organized labour, setting up of unions will create more opportunities to bargain collectively for better working conditions. Such changes will produce a labour force that is better educated, more diverse, safer, and working under better conditions today than in pre-independent era.

b. History of Child Labour

The early view of child labour was largely based on English industrial revolution. It was believed in 17th century, that idle children were a source of crime and poverty. To combat such idleness, apprenticeships were introduced for children of working-class. Child labour was not seen as exploitation of child, but rather often considered as an act of charity.

Children labour continued as a normal practice till early 20th century. With the rise of the industrial revolution, more children were being used in production with no pay and thus get exposed to the workplace hazards of factory at a very early age. The American, for example, start legislating abolition of child labour in 1916, with the Keating-Owen Child Labour Act. This Act banned the sale of products manufactured with the labour of any child under age fourteen (14) and heavily restricted child labour under age of sixteen (16). This Act could not last long in the hands factories owners, who challenged Keating–Owen Act and in 1918, the Supreme Court of United States of America declared the Act unconstitutional and thus overturned it.

c. Racial equality

Racial equality has long been a growing concern in Europe and United States. In United States, African-Americans, in particular, have struggled to gain equality in a variety of areas including employment. During the Civil

Rights Movement of the 1960s, protestors engaged in a persistent campaign of demonstrations, inform of marches, sit-ins, and freedom journeys. These activities drew national attention to the fact that racial discrimination is still prevalent in many areas, including workplace.

Only after the post-WWII, the laws designed to prohibit employers from discriminating along racial lines started to be enact. In United States, the Civil Rights Act of 1964 was passed, making it illegal for employers to discriminate on the basis of race.

In 1960s – 1970s, European socialisation movement started. Young people started demanding more equality for all and thus equal pay for the same job. Such demonstrations were also carried out in forms of marches, sit-ins and huge protest that would result into cities lockdown. These activities have also drawn governments attention to the fact that racial discrimination is still prevalent and thus leads to enactment of better labour laws.

These movements culminated in the establishment of International Labour Organisation as United Nations Agency for Labour.

d. Working conditions

Generally, the legislative enacted for better labour conditions have created safer working environments for all. In the early 20th century, few rules and standards attempted to regulate health and safety in the workplace. However, lack of national and international labour regulations, combined with unresponsive national legal system, left employees with little legal options when injured at work. It was only after the national governments enacted laws that safeguard the employees' right to compensation and occupational safety and health, when working conditions became safer for workers. Such laws were not achieved with ease, but hard fought.

To illustrate, please see President Theodore Roosevelt argument in favour of workers' compensation:

Theodore Roosevelt, arguing in favour of workers' compensation (then known as workmen's compensation) laws in 1913, where he offered the story of an injured worker that summed up the legal recourse available for workplace injuries at the time. The uncovered gears of a grinding machine ripped off a woman's arm. She had complained earlier to her employer that state law required the gears be covered. Her employer responded that she could either do her job or leave. Under the prevailing common-law rules of negligence, because she continued working she had assumed the risk of the dangerous condition and was not entitled to compensation for her injury.

As illustrated above, common-law negligence was not ideal for handling employment injuries. Employees who saw danger at work could either "assume the risk" and continue working, or leave work. Employees were powerless to change the working condition.

e. *Source of Labour Law*

Like any other field of law, the sources of labour law are:

- Constitution;
- Labour Act, 2017;
- Collective Agreements;
- Contract of employment;
- Supranational Conventions / Treaties;
- Custom Practice.

I.IV Basic Conditions at Workplace

a. *Probation*

Employers use probationary periods to coach and evaluate new employees, employees placed in a new position, and employees with performance problems. A probationary period is a useful management tool, but it can also cause legal trouble. Below, we explain how and when to use probationary periods in a way that would not bring problems to employer.

A probationary period is a stretch of time during which a new or existing employee receives extra supervision and coaching, either to learn a new job or to turn around a performance problem. The probationary period can be as short as a month or as long as a year, depending on the situation.

Employers may require probationary periods for:

- new employees i.e. an introductory probation;
- current employees who are promoted to a new position i.e. an introductory probation; or
- current employees with significant performance problems i.e., performance probation.

The purpose of a probationary period is to suspend or modify the usual employment rules for an employee who is learning a job or struggling to perform. For an introductory probation, the employee is placed on probation for three or six months defending on the reasonable period in accordance with labour market rules.

For performance introductory probation, the employee is placed on probation for three or six months defending on the reasonable period in accordance with labour market rules. During this period, the employee will meet with his or her supervisor each week to review progress on the monthly reports and go over questions and concerns. The supervisor will provide detailed feedback and coaching. If the employee can't improve during the probationary period, he or she will be fired. Hence if the company decides to use a probationary period, it should take steps to make sure that employees know they can still be fired at any time.

A probationary period can be a useful coaching tool; because it gives a struggling employee some extra time and supervision while learning a new job. However, it can also lead to legal trouble if it compromises at-will employment.

Employment at-will means that the employer may fire the employee at any time, for any reason that is not illegal (for example, due to race or gender discrimination). However, an employer can lose this right if it makes a promise that isn't consistent with at-will employment (to learn more, see At-Will Employment).

The implied promise (or threat) of a probationary period is that the employee will have the benefit of that stretch of time to learn a new job or improve at an old one. In other words, it could indicate that the employee will have the full probationary period to get up to speed and would not be fired during that time. Likewise, an employee may expect that he or she will continue to be employed if he or she successfully completes the probationary period.

In order to avoid any problems with employment at-will, all employment documents that reference the probationary period, including the employee handbook, performance appraisals, performance improvement plans, hiring paperwork, should clearly state that the probationary period does not change the at-will employment relationship. These documents should clearly state that an employee might still be fired for any reason at any time, during the probationary period or after completing it.

In addition to the above, be clear about probationary expectations. Notify the employee of the probationary status, i.e. how long it will last, and what are the requirements to be met during that period. What will be the supervisory meetings schedules? It is advisable to conduct periodical reviews with the employee to provide feedback and counselling. If the employee is having performance issues, give detailed guidance on how the employee can improve and offer some training, if necessary. Assign a knowledgeable and experienced mentor to advise the employee. If the employee needs training or other resources, make sure they are provided. Get feedback from human resources department. Human resource can help in finding solutions that are aimed treating the employee fairly and consistently. For example, if a struggling employee is placed on a one-month probationary period, the employer must want to make sure he/she is giving the employee a fair chance to turn things around. To avoid legal trouble, clearly document everything during the probationary period: the employee's performance, employer efforts to coach and manage, any training provided etc.

b. Leaves

Not all employees jump at the chance to take their annual leave for various reasons, including fear of falling behind at work or disappointing their manager. However, employees who take adequate time to rest make for a healthy business and taking leave should be encouraged. Here's why:

(i) Stress and fatigue busting

By taking a break, employees get a chance to re-energise their mind and body. Studies shows that after a holiday, employees are less stressed and can manage work more responsibly and efficiently. Its highlight the fact that this system is rotational so everyone feels his or her turn will come.

(ii)   Increased productivity and creativity

A rested mind and body boosts productivity and creativity – and allows employees to approach tasks with better perspective and a fresh mind-set. Recognise hard work and targets met by offering incentives that extend annual leave (bonus leave days). Giving an extra annual leave day on an employee's birthday or offering a half day for overtime worked highlights the importance of taking time off to recharge.

(iii)   Decline in absenteeism

Annual leaves contributed to a business well-being. A healthy and happy employee is less likely to be absent on an on-going basis. By stipulating a date by which employees should use their leave, the Human Resources Department should remind employees to book for busy periods like school or summer holidays in advance to ensure they get their rest at the most opportune time. Consider closing shop during a major holiday period, if possible, encouraging all employees to take leave at that time.

(iv)   More highs than lows

Research shows that recharging personnel promotes a positive outlook toward new projects and challenges. Moreover, this positivity is often transferable and can be felt throughout the business if all employees have rest and regain the energy they need. Instil a holiday-friendly atmosphere by responding positively when an employee applies for leave. They're less likely to apply for leave if they feel it's frowned upon or 'subtly' discouraged.

(v)   *Improve* prioritisation

A well-organised leave process teaches employees and employers to prioritise effectively. With a common goal in mind, both parties put in the required effort to make things work better. Cut it short – if employees have to jump through hoops to get leave, e.g., filling out extensive forms, providing three months' notice or waiting on and phoning HR for confirmation, becomes time-consuming and irritating. Keeping an organised and efficient system with instant reply is the best.

In conclusion, it is important to keep an eye on your employees' workload, to ensure they have enough time to meet their responsibilities and take their full annual leave. A happy team is more engaged and likely to view their jobs as meaningful work that can be pursued for the long term.

CHAPPTER TWO

Contract of Employment

Labour law does not differ from other laws when coming to contract. However, the employment contract is a legal act, which is not subject to formal requirements. It may be oral, written or electronic. It can also arise tacitly, when an employer allows an employee to work for him. A contract of employment is an agreement between an employer and employee and it is the basis of the employment relationship between the two parties, which contains some legal terms such as:

a. **Statutory** terms: are imposed, varied or regulated by law such as the minimum statutory notice period, e.g. working hours.

b. **Expressed** terms: these are terms that have been specifically mentioned, either in writing or orally, and have been agreed by both employer and employee, e.g. how much one should be getting as monthly salary.

c. **Implied** terms: these are terms that are not set out in writing or agreed orally, but may be too obvious to need to be recorded. An example of this may be that the employee will not steal from the employer, e.g. it is prohibited to steal at work.

d. **Incorporated** terms: are things that have been put into contracts from work rules or collective agreements, e.g. internal rules and regulations.

Therefore, the central doctrine of law of contract, which runs through the contract of employment, is the parties are free to make their own contracts. Such freedom in making of contract is worded better in section 30 of

Contract Act, 2008 that says:

An agreement is not a contract where the parties do not intend to be legally bound by it, and such intend is deemed to be legally binding where the agreement is not caused by:

a. coercion;

b. undue influence;

c. fraud;

d. misrepresentation of situation/facts; or

e. mistake.

So a contract of employment is an agreement made with the free consent of parties with capacity to enter into contract, for a lawful consideration, with a lawful object and with the intention to be legally bound.[16]

a. Status of Contracts of Employment

Employers legally engage employees on either contracts of service or contracts for services. A person engaged under a contract of service is considered to be an employee and therefore protected by the variety of employment legislation; while an independent contractor or self-employed person considered to be under a contract for services with the party for whom the work is being carried out. The distinction between a contract of service, on the one hand, and a contract for services, on the other, is very paramount, because it determines the statutory protection that applies to a person in question. It is sometimes unclear but the type of contract a person is engaged under can have serious implications for both employer and

---

[16] Contract Act, 2008, section 6.

employee in matters such as employment protection, legal responsibilities for injuries caused to members of the public, taxation and social welfare.

To mention but a few: the rights and remedies provided for under the unfair dismissals regulations only apply to employees under a contract of service. Likewise of importance is the fact that employers are only vicariously liable for torts committed by employees who are under a contract of service. Independent contractors under a contract for services, on the other hand, are responsible for their own torts.

There are three conditions that must be fulfilled in order to establish a contract of service:

a. There must be an obligation of the person to provide work in return for a wage or other remuneration;

b. There must be a sufficient degree of control by the employer; and

c. The other provisions of the contract must not be inconsistent with its being a contract of service.

In conclusion, each of these contracts, both parties have specific rights and responsibilities, which differ according to the sort of contract in place.

b. Type of Contract of Employment

Depending on needs, companies may employ on part-time, fixed-term or permanent basis.

(i) Part-time Contract

A part-time employee is an employee who works for fewer hours than a full-time employee doing the same type of work. It is prohibited to treat a part-time employee less favourably than a full-time employee in respect of condition of employment and employee protection applies to part-time employees in the same manner as it applies to full-time employees. A part-time employee may only be treated in a less favourable manner than a full-time employee where such treatment can be justified on objective grounds. It is obvious that a part-timer may receive less salary than a full-timer and that does not lead to labour discrimination. A part-time employee can be either employed under a fixed-term or indefinite contract.

Employers often hire permanent part-timers to avoid including them in company-paid health insurance plans, thereby making them an attractive proposition for budget-constrained firms. However, according to Matthew Struck, a founding partner at Treadstone Risk Management, in Morristown, New Jersey; many employers don't realize hiring permanent part-timers does come with the same legal requirements as permanent full-time employees.

Keeping in mind that anyone who works for an average of thirty (30) hours per week or hundred and thirty (130) hours a month is deemed full time by the Labour Act, 2017. It is however, the opinion of the writer that all permanent part-timers be covered by workers' compensation as part of company's property and work related injuries insurance. Therefore, it would be a criminal offend if a company do not disclose the part-time workers at the time it purchase insurance which shall constitute insurance fraud.

As part-time is attractive to the employers, it also has disadvantages and one example of the said drawback is confidentiality. According to Ken Taber, an employment attorney at Pillsbury Winthrop Shaw Pittman in New York City, permanent part-timers with highly specialized expertise, say, in finance or business law, are privy to significant amounts of confidential information about company, which they may intentionally or inadvertently disclose to competitors. So in order to prevent any diversion of business by such part-timers, it is advisable to have them sign a non-disclosure agreement that, if violated, may result in legal action by the company.

(ii)   Fixed Term Contract

A fixed-term employee is an employee who is employed under a contract which contains a specific starting and ending date or who is employed to carry out a specific task or project or the continuity of contingent on a particular event such as the availability of funding from third party.

It is legally prohibited to keep employee(s) on a basis of fixed-term contracts indefinitely. For instance, if an employee whose employment has continues for two (2) years service as a fixed term employee, when that employee's contract comes up for renewal, the employee can only be offered one further fixed-term contract[17]. Such a renewal on a further fixed-term basis cannot be for more than one year. After this, if the employer wishes the employee to continue, then the employee must be offered an employment on the basis of a contract of indefinite duration.

Equally like part-time employee, a fixed-term employee cannot be treated in a less favourable manner than permanent employee in respect to all rules of employees' protection, other than that relating to unfair dismissal, applies to fixed-term employees in the same manner as it applies to a permanent employee.

a.   Justification for a Fixed-Term Contract[18]

The Employment Contract Act 2014 of Finland presented more

---

[17] Section 29(2) of the Sudanese Labour Act, 1997.
[18] Finish Employment Contract Act 2014.

comprehensive justification for fixed term contract and as such, the author opted to fully use the paragraph here below.

Employment contracts are usually valid indefinitely. Contracts can be made fixed-term on the initiative of the employer only for a justified reason. The provision does not prevent the contracting parties from making a fixed-term contract in cases referred to in the Act[19] if working life needs so require. Fixed- term employment contracts cannot, however, be used to evade the provisions on protection against unilateral termination.

The employment contract can be made fixed-term on the basis of the nature of the work, the fact that the employee works as a substitute or trainee, or for another comparable reason. It can also be made fixed-term for some other reason related to the work or the operation of the enterprise. The reason may be, for example, that the work or work entity which has been done is separately specified and done only once during the operation of the enterprise, or requires special skills. A valid reason can also be that a specific order is being prepared or delivered, or that the work was required to cope with some other kind of peak period. These grounds are valid only if the employer is not able to have the work done by permanent employees. A fixed-term employment contract can also be drawn up for seasonal work. However, if an employer successfully hires an employee to perform a specific job, and the employment lasts for e.g. nine or ten months a year, there is no justification for the employer drawing up fixed-term employment contracts.

A fixed-term employment contract may be made with a substitute

---

[19] Although the Act stands here for Finland Employment Act 2014, it should also be read as Labour Act, 2017 of the Republic of South Sudan. This is because, the author is convinced that the historical and socio-economic factors that have contributed to the enactment of the Labour Act, 2017 cannot be treated to far for the content of the Finish justification for the fixed term contract of employment.

employee for the period of absence of a permanent employee. The duties of the substitute must be specified. However, the duties of the temporarily absent employee do not have to be performed by the substitute but can instead be redistributed by making different internal arrangements.

b. *What is the rationale behind restriction on fixed term*

Fixed-term contracts on another hand are illegal when drawn up for the same job repeatedly and consecutively between the same parties without the justified reason referred to in the paragraph above and legislation. Each fixed-term employment contract has to be drawn up for a justified reason. The employer should evade the protection provided for indefinite employment contracts by use of consecutive fixed-term contracts. If the employer's need for labour is considered to be permanent, then there is no justification for consecutive fixed-term contracts for the same work.

Legally and policy-wise, employers are not allowed to conclude consecutive fixed-term contracts with different employees if the job requires permanent labour. In case of South Sudan, the legal basis is not in the Labour Act, 2017 and for that matter, custom practice form the legal ground for the prohibition of the consecutive fixed term contract of employment. Some may question the use of custom practice as legal ground, but given the fact judicial rulings were once issued in support of the prohibition, make it relevant to conclude so.

The assessment of whether or not fixed-term contracts are appropriate for the job takes into account not only each fixed-term contract individually but also the employer's use of labour for the job in general. If the number of repeated fixed-term contracts, signed either consecutively or frequently, or the combined length of the fixed-term contracts implies that the labour requirement for a job has become permanent, the use of fixed-term contracts for the job is no longer allowed.

(iii)   *Permanent Contract*

Permanent contract is without ending period and it can also be part-time. One should clarify the term "permanent" because it may mislead the students. Permanent contract is not for life, which may end with death of the employee (it is possible for death that is not related with old). Thus this type of employment contract does end with the attainment of the pensionable age, which is in accordance with law that regulate pensionable age in the Country. As indicated in the explanation of the other type of employment contracts above, the employees on permanent employment contracts basis eligible for full employee benefits offered by the employer in accordance with labour law. This can vary for fixed-term contracts, which is determined by the employer.

II.I Formation of Contract of Employment

The Labour Act does not define what a contract of employment is, but defines an employee and employer. The formation of the contract is where the contractual obligation begins. If no contract is formed, neither of the parties can be under any contractual obligations. Therefore, it is very important to have an understanding of each part of a contract's formation. Here below are four basic requirements for formation of contracts:

a. Offer

b. Acceptance

c. Certainty & Intention to Create Legal Relations

d. Consideration & Promissory Estoppel

a. *Offer*

The offer is the first core requirement of the formation of a contract. An understanding of this requirement is vital for learning contract law. Despite an 'offer' being a seemingly simple term, an offer will not always be explicit, and at this point it is the job of the courts to identify what does and does not constitute an offer.

If there is no offer, the other parts of the contract will not operate, this is why it is so important to be able to understand what an offer is.

What makes an offer?

The first requirement of a legally binding agreement as stated above is an offer. One party is the offeror, who presents the offer, and one party is the offeree, who is the potential acceptor of the offer.

The case of *Storer vs. Manchester City Council [1974] 1 WLR 1403* outlines that an offer is:

- An expression of willingness to contract on specified terms; and

- With the intention that it is to be binding once accepted.

Offer vs. Invitation to Discuss

An important distinction to make in contract law is that between an offer and an invitation to discuss. An invitation to discuss can be defined as an indication that a party is open to negotiation.

The case of *Gibson vs. Manchester City Council [1979] 1 WLR 294* held the following statement to be an invitation to negotiate *"May be prepared to sell the house to you"*.

Therefore an invitation of a resume or dinner with an employer in relation to possible vacant post can be treated as an invitation to talk and offer.

Here below are some key distinctions between an offer and an invitation to negotiate:

Offer

- Certain promise to be bound
- Clear and specified terms
- The conduct or words of the party show certainty
- There is no room for negotiation

Invitation to discuss

- There is room for negotiation
- There is an invitation for offers
- There is a request for information
- Lack of certainty

Presumptions

Throughout the history of contract law, there have been various disputes over the distinction between an offer and an invitation to discuss. Therefore, in order to provide a certain degree of clarity, there are a number of presumptions, which are relatively connected to contract of employment and that are applied to certain types of each conduct mentioned above and they are:

Advertisements

As a general rule, the case of *Partridge vs. Crittenden [1968] 2 All ER 421* rules that an advertisement is an invitation to negotiate. The supporting reason for this is the "multi-acceptance" principle.

The *multi-acceptance principle* states: If an advertisement is considered an offer, theoretically, an unlimited amount of people could accept that offer, which causes obvious problems when the advertisement is for a limited amount of positions – for example, as the employer would be in breach of contract to each individual whom they could not offer job.

The argument behind the *multi-acceptance principle* is: following this argument, it is obvious that an advertisement does not fulfil the requirement from *Storer vs. Manchester City Council*, as there is clearly no unequivocal exhibition of contractual intent; therefore the reasonable person would recognize that the institution who placed the advertisement never intended to contract with everybody who responds to the advertisement.

Exceptions to advertisements as invitations to negotiate: one hypothetical argument suggests that an advertisement from a manufacturer may be construed as an offer, as the manufacturer would be able to make more of the item in question in response to all of the acceptances. This is not a rule, but may be a factor in a court's decision.

b. Acceptance

There are many different ways an offer can be accepted. It is very important for a student to be able to differentiate between the different rules that govern acceptance.

Acceptance precedes an offer as the second requirement for a legally binding contract. Acceptance can be defined as the core requirement in contractual formation where the parties' intentions as to the terms of the contract are the same or unequivocal. This intent must be effectively communicated to the offeror to complete the acceptance of the offer.

Unequivocal is the first key terms when dealing with issues of acceptance.

34

It is seen as "leaving no doubt" and is often strictly interpreted - *Hyde vs. Wrench [1840] 3 Beav 334.*

Communication is the second key word. Intent must be communicated effectively to avoid overlooking of the issues.

Acceptance must mirror the offer

Often in situations where it seems as an offeree has effectively communicated his/her acceptance of an offer to the offeror. If this acceptance however has modified conditions attached as to the terms of the offer, then do we still considered this unequivocal?

Counter-offers

In *Hyde vs. Wrench [1840] 3 Beav 334*, the above issue was raised in the Court with the following facts:

An offeror made an offer to sell land at £1000 and the offeree responded by attempting to accept the offer at £950. This was subsequently rejected by the offeror. An attempt was later made by the offeree to accept the original offer of £1000.

The Court found that the original offeree was now unable to accept the original offer of £1000. This was drawn from the fact that the previous "acceptance" of the offer at £950 had fundamentally changed the initial offeror position. Why? When the offeree changed the conditions of the offer by changing the terms of its price, he in fact created a counter-offer. Counter-offers revoke any previous offers and a revoked offer is not capable of being accepted.

Cross-offers

It is incredibly rare; however there are instances where two parties both send complimentary offers to one-another at the same time. The question is, if this occurs has the contract been accepted?

In the Case: *Tinn vs. Hoffman (1873) 29 LT 271* – Such instances are not sufficient to amount to the acceptance of either offer i.e. offers and acceptance must be communicated separately.

c. *Certainty & Intention to Create Legal Relations*

An agreement may not qualify as a valid and enforceable contract if it lacks certainty, however, not all agreements are legally binding or have an intention to create legal relations.

Certainty

Once an offer and acceptance are considered valid, an agreement is formed. Certainty will be the next requirement to make the agreement legally enforceable. In case the agreement is not considered certain and thus lacks the contractual requirement of certainty then it will not be enforceable - *Gunthing vs. Lynn (1831) 2 B7 Ad 232.*

Any case involving a dispute as to whether a contract lacks certainty is a fact based and discrete. As such, it is always important to pay close attention to the facts surrounding the agreement, and any clauses or wording relating to the said agreement.

The two areas that need to be considered when reviewing whether an agreement is certain are: (a) whether the agreement is vague and (b) whether the agreement is incomplete.

Resolving vagueness

Use of business customs and trade usages: in the interest of contractual and commercial certainty, a Court may often give effect to vague agreements by filling gaps with business, customs and trade usages. The Case in point: *Courtney vs. Fairbairn Ltd vs. Tolaini Bros (Hotels) Ltd [1975] 1 All ER 453*.

Reasonableness: when a contract fail through virtue of an uncertainty the Court may apply an objective standard to fix the issue. A good illustrative case would be *Hillas & Co vs. Arcos Ltd (1932) 147 LT 503*.

In this case, a contract was made for the supply of goods described as "fair". As "fair" in terms of goods is not an adequate description, the Court applied an objective assessment and determined that "fair" in the context of the agreement could be adequately defined.

Doctrine of severability: in case one of the clauses is irreconcilable with the agreement due to vagueness of it, the Court may completely strike it off from the agreement so the rest of the said agreement can be legally enforced. In *ERJ Lovelock vs. Exportles [1968] 1 Lloyd's Rep 163*, the Court ruled: if a phrase contradicts itself then the Court may remove it from the agreement.

Incompleteness

An agreement does not require every minute detail to be addressed for it to be capable of legal enforceability. Every essential piece of information however is required - *Grow With Us Ltd vs. Green Thumb (UK) Ltd [2006] EWCA Civ 1201*.

The degree to which a term is considered essential within an agreement varies depending on the facts surrounding the agreement.

It is therefore, prudent to pay attention to the facts when before concluding the incompleteness of a contract. The key point to consider is the extent to which a term is in fact vital to the agreement.

Resolving incompleteness

Determination by contracting party: If a term within a contract is missing e.g. salary or duty to be executed, then yet, there may be a clause in the contract that permits a particular party to resolve the issue - *Bulk Trading Co v Zenziper Grains and Feedstuffs [2001] 1 Lloyd's Rep 357* is the Case in point.

Determination by a third party: in case a situation arises where a contract is incomplete by a lack of terms due to a third-party requirement or expertise needed to activate a certain issue/duty, such as an independent safety expert. The Court may ensure that this term is given effect in order to ensure the contract is provided with its missing terms - *Sudbrook Trading Estate v Eggleton [1983] 1 AC 444 is the Case in point.*

Intention to create legal relations

The intention to create legal relations is the requirement that parties to the agreement wish to achieve. It was said earlier on that not all contracts/agreements are legally binding.

There is a serious discourse amongst different legal school of thoughts surrounding the concept of requiring intention to create legal relations. Williston a leading scholar argued that *animus contrahendi* as a concept is a product of Continental jurisprudence and that it should be excised from the common law as alien and unnecessary, since there already exists another test of legal enforceability: the doctrine of consideration. Once consideration has been shown to exist, he further argued, it no longer matters what the parties themselves may have thought about questions of legal enforceability.

The Courts in response have adopted an objective based test of reasonableness to determine whether parties intended to be legally bound by the agreement or not.

The reasonableness test

The test of whether there was an intention to create legal relation during formation of contract is called the *Test of Reasonableness.* When an enforcement of contract arise on ground of an intention to create legal relations, the Court does not look into the subjective opinions of the parties, but rather take an objective assessment of the situation in which the contract arose. Such objective assessment is determined by the stand of "reasonable man" then - *Smith vs. Hughes (1871) LR 6 QB 597.* The assessment question is: whether or not the parties would have reasonably believed themselves to be entering into a contract, of which failure to adhere to, would have legal repercussions - *Albert vs. Motor Insurer's Bureau [1972] AC 301.*

d. Consideration & Promissory Estoppel

This paragraph will explain two principles of law of contract. The first of these two principles is consideration, which along with the offer, acceptance and intention to create legal relations, form a legally binding contract. Promissory Estoppel is a related principle, which can act as an *exception* to the main rules of consideration. That is mean, for a consideration to be valid it must have economic value and should involve an exchange of benefit between the parties.

The question whether the parties met the consideration conditionality during formation of contract is one of the fundamental steps in determining the enforceability of a contract.

Currie vs. Misa (1874) LR 10 Ex 153 defined consideration as:

"A valuable consideration, in the sense of the law, may consist either in some right, interest, profit, or benefit accruing to the one party, or some forbearance, detriment, loss, or responsibility, given, suffered, or undertaken by the other."

Based on the *Currie vs. Misa* ruling, we can conclude that consideration is essentially the exchange of benefits between parties.

Now the following question is: does the exchange of the promise to a benefit constitute valid consideration? It would be a blunder to believe that the consideration must itself transfer to form a binding contract. A promise to transfer such consideration is often considered as sufficient and this assertion was confirmed in *Dunlop vs. Selfridge Ltd [1915] AC 847*, where Lord Dunedin stated that promises were indeed considered enforceable.

Promissory estoppel

Promissory estoppel is an equitable remedy that prevents a party from rescinding a promise made earlier. Be warns that the concept is not just about preventing the rescission of a promise, but it encompasses more. The Court set in the *Central London Property Trust Ltd vs. High Trees House Ltd [1947] KB 130* the test as to whether promissory estoppel will apply in a situation where a promise has been rescinded or not and the requirements be met are:

- There must have been an existing legal relationship between the parties;
- The promissory estoppel should not create new legal

relationship if it did not exist, as affirmed by Lord Denning in *Combe vs. Combe [1951] 2 KB*;

- There must have been a reliance on the promise; and
- The promisee must rely on the promisors' promise in order to attempt to apply promissory estoppel. This means that by relying on the promise the actions of the promisee must have changed.

There is a legal discourse on the threshold of the aforementioned test set by *Central London Property Trust Ltd vs. High Trees House Ltd [1947] KB 130*. The threshold of the test is measured by some legal scholars as low and thus they argued that a detriment should be required in order to establish reliance, however both cases of *Central London Property Trust Ltd vs. High Trees House Ltd [1947] KB 130* and *Combe vs. Combe [1951] 2 KB*, disputed the requirement of a detriment. In *Combe vs. Combe [1951] 2 KB*, the Court applied the famous "equitable maxim" which literally mean that equity *sees that as done what ought to be done*, therefore promissory estoppel can only be used as a "shield not a sword". In line with above Court reasoning we can conclude that promissory estoppel cannot be used as a cause of action, but only as a defence.

A case which provides a good example of this is The Post Chaser [1982] 1 All ER 19, in which the promise was revoked within a few days, due to this small lapse in time, the promise would not have relied upon their promise or changed their position, therefore, it was equitable to allow the promisor rescind on the promise.

II.II Content of the Contract of Employment

Since one is now acquainted of the basic requirements that make up an employment contract as mentioned in II.I above: e.g. offer, acceptance, consideration and capacity to intention to create legal relations. However, all of the aforementioned requirements don't address the content of the contract of employment. So the question is: What is the content of the contract of employment? The adaptability of a contract of employment to conform to changing circumstances is seen as an advantage. Having said that, the fundamental terms to be in the contract of employment are:

- date of commencement of the work,
- duration of the contract of employment and the justification for a fixed term: in case of fixed term employment relationship,
- probation period,
- the work/duty station,
- employee's principle duties (terms of reference),
- the remuneration and the pay period,
- regular working hours,
- manner of determining leaves and the period of notice, and
- the collective agreement applicable to the work.

Job Description

The contract should include a job description. It is good to have written documentation of what has been agreed on job, because it helps during employment dispute. It also helps the supervisor in holding an employee accountable of his/her shortcoming and likewise for the employee holding an employer accountable of his/her shortcoming on his/her duties.

Location of Work

Monthly remuneration and daily allowances are calculated on the basis of agreed work location. Location of work is the locality where employees predominantly performed their work.

Duration of Employment

It is now known fact that contract of an employment may be temporary or permanent. Every contract of employment must always include a termination clause to enable the parties to terminate the contract within the agreed term of notice. Dismissal of the employee from the duty may terminate a contract of employment, but not always. In order to protect the employees' job security, the employers must have an acceptable reason for offering a temporary contract, as seen above. It can be, for example, seasonal nature of work or substituting another employee during leave.

Collective Agreement

Collective agreements become part of the contract of employment and that mean all the conditions thereof, such as salary increment or holiday pay, become part of the employment contract. It is always advisable to check the contents of your employment contract to ensure that you are aware of your rights.

Probationary Period

The maximum duration of probationary period is six (6) months, but the practice is three (3) months. The employer may not extend the length of the probationary period even if the employee is absent from work during probationary period. This is regardless of incapacity for work due to sickness or injury, or due to parental leave unless the injury is industrial one. In case of a temporary contract of less than 12 months, the probationary period may not be longer than two (2) weeks.

Termination of Contract during the Probationary Period

During the probationary period, the parties to the employment contract may terminate the contract without notice. This means that an employment relationship is duly terminated on the day of notification of termination. It is not permissible to terminate the employment relationship on the basis of probationary condition until work has commenced.

Payment of Salary (Section 49 of Labour Act, 2017)

The amount of pay, period of pay and payment date should be agreed upon and put in writing. In addition to monetary compensation, pay may include fringe benefits such as communications allowance.

All contractual benefits in addition to monthly salary should be included in the employment contract or in its attachment. It is particularly important to agree on the payment of performance-related pay or bonuses at the termination of the employment contract.

Minimum Wages (Section 50 of Labour Act, 2017)

Payment of salaries should be done on the basis of respecting the country's minimum wages standard. South Sudan minimum is to be determines by the Council of Ministers upon the recommendation by the competent authority, in this case: Labour Commission and Ministry of Labour. The Council in determining the minimum wages may task the competent authority to review, adjust and fix the minimum wages. In doing so, the competent authority should take into account the following elements:

    a.   the basic needs of the employees;

    b.   the general level of wages/salaries in the Country;

    c.   the cost of living and changes in such cost;

    d.   the level of productivity; and

    e.   any other that Council may deemed fit.

This process is subject to periodical review at least after every two years.

Promotion of Equal Payment (Section 50(3) of the Labour Act, 20170

The Council of Ministers may recommend to the competent authority to fix different minimum wages/salaries for different occupations or special categories of employees. However, this process should be done without contravening the principle of equal pay for equal work. The principle of equal pay is also paramount when coming to equal pay between man and woman for equal work. In conclusion, the hourly minimum wage/salary should be one-eighth of any daily wage/salary fixed and the Ministry shall publish the minimum wage/salary in the official gazette or any public media as the Competent Minister may determine.

Working Hours (Section 56 of Labour Act, 2017)

The employee's regular working hours and the application of Section 56 of Labour Act, 2017 shall be agreed upon in the employment contract. The Labour Act stipulates that overtime shall be compensated by overtime pay as defined by law. Agreed upon separately, overtime may be compensated by corresponding leave. Unless otherwise agreed, overtime must be compensated in monetary pay. Compensatory overtime must be ordered by the employer and agreed by the employee.

Work of CEO or comparable work which can be regarded as independent work on the basis of its duties or the position of the employee in the organisation, and which explicitly corresponds the leading of the company, organisation, fund and or an independent part thereof, remains outside the scope of the overtime.

Leave and Holiday Pay

Annual leave is accrued according to Section 60 of Labour Act, 2017.

In general, an employee is entitled to 1.5–2 days annual leave for each full month at work. In situation where the employee has outstanding annual leave at termination of the employment contract, the accrued leave should be paid as holiday compensation with the final pay.

National holidays pay is as well a statutory benefit in South Sudan. Normal holiday pay is however not a statutory benefit. It has to be agreed upon separately, either in collective agreement or in the employment contract.

Notice of Termination of Employment Contract

Term of notice may be agreed on, irrespective of the duration of employment and this may be applied a long term to the employer than to the employee. However, Section 72 of the Labour Act, 2017 prescribed the notification period as table 2 here below:

Tab. 2

Duration of Employment	Section 72 required Period of Notice
One (1) year or more	One (1) month notification
Six (6) months or more	Fourteen (14) days notification
Less than six 96) months	Seven (7) days notification

Non-compete Clause

A non-compete clause (NCC) prevents an employee from pursuing a similar profession or trade in competition against the employer (usually in post-employment). Non-competition clauses are used to discourage an employee from working for a competitor using the specialized knowledge, skills, or confidential information gained while working for the employer. A non-compete clause may be agreed on when possibilities of strong arguments related to the activities of the employer and the nature of the employment relationship exists. In these cases, the type of employer activities, need for protection and the position and duties of the employee are taken into account. Another mean of blocking possible post-employment in the same field, is to include in NCC the number of years which an employee must observes before joining any employer of the business nature as his/her previous employer. To be applicable, a non-compete clause has to be explicitly agreed upon before the employment commences or during the employment. In general, a non-compete clause restricts, within agreed time limits, the leaving employee to be employed in competing companies or embarking on a competing business of his or her own.

There is no statutory limit or maximum length of a non-compete clause in South Sudan Labour Act; however, practice range between six (6) and twelve (12) months. The employee will not be bound by the non-compete clause if the employment relationship is terminated for reasons originating from the employer. It is advisable that employees let their NCC checked by their lawyers, so you know what you are committing yourself to.

Non-disclosure Agreement (NDA)

Traditionally, the employment contract stipulates that the employee may not disclose confidential or proprietary information or trade secrets of the employer to any third party during the employment. Even after termination of employment, the employee may not, without permission, disclose any of the above-mentioned information to third party. Disclosure of business-sensitive information is a punishable act during the employment and some years after the termination according Criminal Code. Employment contracts often include a separate clause on non-disclosure.

The idea of non-disclosure is to protect the trade secrets of not only the employer but also those of other companies, its customers or business partners. In a well-written non-disclosure clause or agreement, the confidential or proprietary information is clearly defined. It is worth mentioning that the obligation of non-disclosure shall not apply to the professional skills or previous experience of the employee.

It is hard to find a codified the contents of non-disclosure clause or agreement. Non-disclosure may have an undetermined duration after the termination of employment. However, it is justified to limit the validity of such agreement to 1 or 2 years after the termination of employment relationship and as the interest to protect confidential, proprietary information or trade secrets decreases over time and disappear altogether.

CHAPTER THREE

Termination of the Contract of Employment

Section[20] 72 of the Labour Act, 2017 stipulates that a contract of employment may be lawfully terminated by notice by either party to the contract. Normally, such a notice of termination is agreed in the contract of employment and the parties to the contract must abide with the agreed notification period.

One may wonder as to why terminate an employment contract. Well, employer always expects employee to serve to satisfactory for a work he/she is contracted to carryout. In addition, employment contract consists of constant relation between the employer and the employee, which needs to be adhered to. Termination of the employment contract would become very significant to understand when it comes to employee and employer relationship issues. In this case, one of the parties would wishes to terminate the employment contract based on a number of grounds, for instance; an employer who aims to terminate an employment relationship as a mean to get rid of employee who became liability.

Having seen the statutory requirement for termination of the employment contract, it is the opinion of the author that contract of employment may be terminated in two ways as below:

---

[20] Section is abbreviated or shorthanded by the small letter "s".

a. Termination with a just Reason by Employer

The termination of the employment contract for an undetermined term by the employer should be subject to existence of just reason. The employer, who want to terminates the contract of an employee who has an indefinite period and is employed in an establishment with thirty or more workers and he/she is in a senior management position for a minimum of six months, must base his/her reason for termination a just ground. Such justification must be found on the capacity or performance of the employee in his/her capacity as a manager. Another justifying reason would be the economic crisis, the closure of the establishment, and interruption of business due to the shortage of raw materials. The aforementioned reasons may indeed result into downsizing of manpower.

A good example for just reasons for termination of the employment contract is incapacity of the employee. This is because the incapacity of the employee would result into professional incompetence or physical incapacity. However, justify reason for termination of employment contract would not contravene a notice periods and the employee should also be compensated for the loss of job. In short, termination of employment contract must be based on valid and justifiable reasons, and it should be consistent with itself, which means that grounds of termination shall be harmonized with demand.

In case of termination of employment contract without justifiable ground, principle evidence rule is usually in favour of employee. The burden of proof is on the employer. If there is no sufficient written evidence in the hands of the employer to terminate the employment contract, then employer action may lead to unjustified termination of employment contract.

b. Termination of Employment Contract by employee

If the employee chooses to cease performing work on receiving notice from the employer, the employer is obliged to pay the employee a sum equal to half the wages that would be payable in respect of the unexpired period of notice.

III.I Failure to give Notice

Notices are means of formal communication targeted at a particular person or a group of persons. It is like a news item informing such person or persons of some important event. This can be an invitation to a meeting, an announcement of any event, to issue certain instructions, make appeals etc.

It is generally written and then displayed at a public place or served to a concern person(s), where it is accessible to all. They can be pasted on notice boards. If it is meant for a wider audience, it can even be published in a newspaper. The government when it issues notices must publish it in national and local papers.

In the labour relationship, if the employer fails to give notice, he/she shall be liable of unfair dismissal and to pay to the employee a sum to be determine by Labour Office in accordance with the provisions of the Labour Act. In case of employee who absent him/herself from work without notice, the employer will have a justifiable ground to terminate the employment contract without notice to the employee, but it should be after the employee was given a reasonable time to resume his/her work; however failed to show up at work. The employer, in that case, will not pay any compensation of non-notification, but pay the normal dues of the employee. An employment can be terminated without notice or obligation to compensate for notice when the length of service is not longer than one month, or when there is a good and sufficient cause e.g. disciplinary action.

III.II Settlement of Outstanding Dues

Without prejudice to what may be due under the law relating to notice, the employee is entitled to be paid all entitlements, on a proportional basis according to the period of employment. Employees who had their employment terminated are to receive remunerations that may be due to them, including wages, overtime payments, statutory bonuses, notice money and monetary settlement of leave not used by the employee. All outstanding wages should be settled by the next pay date following the termination of employment. An employee who is not paid for his/her work or does not receive his/her wage on time must first bring this to the attention of his employer. If the employer persists in not issuing the payment due, the employee can report the matter to the Labour Office for action.

III.III What is Unfair Dismissal?

Unfair dismissal is when an employee is dismissed from their job in a harsh, unjust or unreasonable manner. A termination of an employee or dismissal may be determined to be unfair, when it is not justified on facts or that the process followed were inadequate or when it was done in a harsh manner in all circumstances of the case. Each termination case relies on its own circumstances.

There are couple of ways a dismissal might actually be a wrongful termination in disguise. The first happens when an employer includes a particular employee in a layoff for illegal reasons. For example, even an employer that has perfectly legitimate economic reasons to lay off employees generally might decide to include a particular employee i.e. because she has complained of sexual harassment, because he has a disability, or because she has exercised a legal right (for example, by taking maternity leave or filing a workers' compensation claim). It doesn't matter that the employer has sound reasons for letting workers go or that some workers may have been laid off for legitimate reasons. If an employee can show that there were illegal reasons why he or she was selected for layoff, that employee may have a wrongful termination claim.

The other way a layoff may constitute wrongful termination is by the impact it has on workplace demographics. If a layoff has a disproportionate negative effect on a protected group (such as youth, women or minority), the employees may be able to prove a disparate impact discrimination claim. In this situation, the employees are not arguing that the employer intentionally selected individual employees for layoff because of, for example, their race.

Instead, the employees claim that the employer's apparently neutral selection criteria screened out too many employees in particular groups and were, therefore, discriminatory.

III.IV Statutory Prohibition of the Termination of Employment Contract

Section 73(2) of the Labour Act, 2017 prohibited the termination of the employment contract on the following grounds:

a. if an employee is a member or participant in any activity of the trade union outside working hours or with the consent of the employer during working hours;

b. if an employee is seeking office as or acting or having acted as representative of other employees at workplace;

c. if employees are filling a complaint or grievance or participating in proceeding against the employer involving an alleged violation of this Act, other laws, regulations or terms of Collective Agreement or Award;

d. any of the grounds of discrimination prohibited by s.6 of Labour Act, 2017;

e. absence of an employee from work for reasons acceptable according to the provisions of Labour Act or authorisation of the employer; or

f. failure by the employer to provide an employee with an entitlement provided for under Labour Act or any other applicable law or Collective Agreement or Arbitration Award.

III.V Termination of Employment Contract on Redundancy

Section 77 of Labour Act, 2017 permit the employer to lay employees off on ground of redundancy because of the change in the operational requirement of the employer. However, the employer should apply for the approval from the Labour Office, when the intended number of the to-be laid-off employees is more than ten (10) within a period of three (3) months. This provision was meant to protect the industrial interest during the economic crisis.

Inclusion, notification of termination of employment contract has a limit. The s.82 of Labour Act, 2017 provided that after the day on which a notice of termination expires and an employer request an employee to remain in employment, or employee continues working without express dissent from the employer. Notice of termination of employment contract shall be deemed to be null and void and so doing the employment contract continues to be valid.

Redundancy is one of the most contested and controversial aspects of employment, especially with regards to economies with unfavourable economic climates. Many employers may sometimes be faced with the unfortunate challenge of instituting changes into their business and their business practices in order to reduce operating costs and inevitably being forced to make redundancies. Perhaps the last thing that a Small to Medium Enterprise (SME) needs in such an event, is to become liable to further expenses due to poor execution of correct redundancy procedures.

In a nutshell, the term "redundancy", in the context of employment law, refers to a scenario wherein an employer reduces their workforce in the event that a certain job/jobs are no longer needed, i.e., they become "redundant". Such situations may arise due to factors that are outside the control of the employee itself, such as, but not limited to, the business closing down, the employer needing to cut expenses, the advent of artificial technology or other technologies that have made that job unnecessary, the job no longer exists, or the business's ownership changing hands, and thus, in most circumstances, redundancy is not a reflection of the employee's ability to do their job, rather it is caused by auxiliary factors.

In most cases apart from the closing down of the business, employers must provide reasonable justification for rendering an employee's position as redundant. It is important to note that redundancy can only take place in the event that the position itself is declared redundant and does not take place if one employee is just replaced with a newer one. Colloquially, the terms redundancy, retrenchment, and layoff are used interchangeably. They can be either of a forced or voluntary nature, with regards to which employees are let go from a firm. In the case of voluntary redundancies, employers usually offer incentives such as severance packages or garden leave. Voluntary redundancies prevent the employer from having to choose which employee to terminate. In the event that voluntary redundancies are unsuccessful, a commonly used technique of *"Last In, First Out"* (LIFO) is employed in forced redundancies, whereby employees who have been with a business for the least amount of time are let go off first.

Other factors that may be used in assessing redundancy possibilities include factors such as attendance records, disciplinary records, the standard of work performance of an employee, the employee's prior experience, or the contribution to the business as a whole. It becomes the onus of the employer to apply the test for redundancy and assess he/she requires fewer employees to carry out a certain piece of work, and not just simply the work becoming diminished or ceased.

Upon the establishment of an act of removal of an employee as a "*dismissal*", a simple test has to be applied to ascertain whether that dismissal qualifies as "*redundancy*". The test, established by various law, entails the following questions:

a. Was the employee in question dismissed?

b. If yes, was the employer's necessity for that certain work to be carried out by the employee ceased or diminished, or was it expected to become ceased or diminished?

c. If so, was the dismissal caused wholly or solely by this aforementioned reason?

This test was primarily set out Employment Appeal Tribunal (EAT), a superior court of record in England, Wales, and Scotland, in the case of *Safeway v Burrell* [1997 UKEAT 168_96_2401 Appeal No. EAT/168/96][21], and was later reaffirmed in the House of Lords

---

[21] Case: *Safeway v Burrell* [1997 UKEAT 168_96_2401 Appeal No.

(HL) case of *Murray & Annor v Foyle Meats* [1999 UKHL 30][22]. On the basis of this test, "transferred redundancies", i.e., situations wherein an employee who was previously not in a situation to fall into redundancy, gets replaced by an employee who was, are deemed lawful. In such situations, employees are *"bumped"* into positions of becoming redundant, the EAT analyses factors such as the employee's capabilities and conduct, that would have led the employee to fall into such a situation. The 2012 case at the EAT of *Packman Lucas Associates v Fauchon* [UKEAT/0017/12/LA][23] established that it was not necessary for the business to have a reduction in the number of employees, that are carrying out a certain piece of work, in order to satisfy the statutory definition of redundancy under *"Employment Rights Act 1996"* (ERA 1996). It is also important to note that should an employer choose not to renew a fixed-term employment contract that covers an absent employee (for

---

EAT/168/96.

[22] Case: *Murray & Annor v Foyle Meats* [1999 UKHL 30].

[23] Case: *Packman Lucas Associates v Fauchon* [UKEAT/0017/12/LA].

example, an employee that is on sick or maternity leave), it would not amount to redundancy under the ERA 1996.

In short, redundancy should be a last resort in an organisation's restructuring. It can be one of the most distressing events an employee can experience. It requires sensitive handling by the employer to ensure fair treatment of the redundant employee as well as the productivity and morale of the remaining workforce. Redundancy legislation is complex, and employers need to understand their obligations, including employees' rights and the correct procedures to follow.

CHAPTER FOUR

Working Conditions, Health and Safety

The working environment must be safe and secure at all time. Both employer and employee must strictly observe the safety at workplace. A poor working conditions can damage employee health and put his/her safety and that of his/her colleagues at risk. The employer is legally responsible for ensuring good working conditions, but employees also have a responsibility to work safely.

Working conditions refers to the working environment and all existing circumstances affecting labour in the workplace, including job hours, physical aspects, legal rights and responsibilities.

So, working conditions means, *"the conditions in which an individual or staff works, including but not limited to such things as amenities, physical environment, stress and noise levels, degree of safety or danger, and the like".*[24]

Working conditions are demands and Firms compete to offer attractive conditions as a means to attract and retain talent in their Firms. The law in many jurisdictions also defines a minimum set of working conditions that employers must provide. Hereunder are the common types of working conditions:

---

[24] http://www.businessdictionary.com/definition/working-conditions.html

Table 3.

Hygiene factors	Health and safety	Remuneration	Profit sharing
Responsibility & accountability	Workload	Work schedule	Occupational stress
Commuting & travel	Autonomy	Controls	Organizational culture
Employee benefits	Work-life balance	Performance management	Job security
Employment terms			

We will give each of the 17 types of working conditions a short explanation and the rest is left to experience in real working-life.

a. Hygiene Factors

Hygiene factors are basic expectations that employees have of a working environment. When these conditions are not met, employees become dissatisfied. For examples, a staff expect to have a somehow comfortable sit or working space and a clean washroom.

b. Health and Safety

A healthy and safe working environment is paramount. Workplace related illness and injury are common problem in many industries. Efforts to make a job healthy and safe include process, standards and safety equipment.

c. Remuneration

A prosperous employment that provides a wage that is competitive given the talent of an individual and the demands of a job. Where working conditions are poor, salary can be increased to serves as compensation. For instant, a position that is stressful may be set at higher pay level than an equivalent position that is not stressful.

d. Profit Sharing

The creation of a plan that allow the employees to share in the success of the company such as the granting of stock to the employees.

e. Employee Benefits

A Firm that has non-wage compensation such as insurance, disability income protection, good pension package, parental leave, day-care, education support, sick leave, house allowances, commuting expenses and wellness program; are well placed and highly appreciated by the employees.

f. Responsibility & Accountability

It is always welcome if the employee knows what his/her responsibilities are, so that he/she knows where he/she can be held accountable for none compliance with the duties.

g. Workload

The intensity and hours of work amount to the workload when not well balanced. For instant, 40 hours of work with light contents such as long meetings as opposed to 50 hours on a factory fast moving assembly line that involves physical exhausting work.

h.   Work Schedule

The employees expect the Manager to have a working schedule for each and every job. The employees prefer standard and predicable working schedule, because it allows them to plan for their social engagements, e.g. family events and activities. Hence, irregular hours that change from week to week basis can decrease employees' satisfaction. Short shifts, overly long shifts and non-standard working hours can be exhausting and disrupt social interaction of the workers.

i.   Occupational Stress

Occupational stress occurs in issues related to workload, schedule, office politics, workplace conflict and inherently stressful activities such as fielding complaints from dissatisfied customers.

j.   Work-Life Balance

We talk of work-life balance when an employee feels that his/her job compliments and supports his/her quality of life opposed to reducing it.

k.   Commuting & Travel

Having a workplace near is the most desirable, because employees commonly find commuting and travel to be stressful. For example, an employee who can walk to work may be more satisfied than an employee who is often stuck in long traffic jam.

l.   Autonomy

The degree of freedom that an employee enjoys at his/her work is called autonomy. It has become a tradition that skill workers are significant freedom to achieves their objectives of their job according their own style and methods.

m. Controls

The employee does internal controls to ensure employee compliance to rules, regulations and norm. Such controls can improve the employee satisfaction if they make workplace more efficient and civil. However, the same controls can be viewed as administrative burden or needless paternalism if they are strict and draconic.

n. Organizational Culture

We talk about the organizational culture when looking at the norms, traditions, expectations and shared values of the Firm that have evolved over of the course of its history. For example, an organization that expects a common courtesy that coercive or rude behaviours are not tolerated, may raise employees' satisfaction.

o. Performance Management

One of the most satisfactory factors for the employees is the process of the setting goals, evaluating performances, rewarding performance, promoting people and handling low performance.

p. Job Security

The likelihood or perceived likelihood that employment will be terminated. Employees become dissatisfied if they feel job insecure. As such an environment stable employment where employees are regularly provided with feedback can improve working conditions.

q. Employment Terms

The employment terms are legal conditions of an employment contract.

For example, non-compete clauses and other terms that restrict employees from compromising the interest of the hiring Firm.

IV.I Health and Safety Regulations

The Workplace Health, Safety and Welfare Regulations lay down minimum standards for workplaces and work in or near buildings. The regulations apply to most types of workplace, however transport, construction sites may have different health and safety regulations. It is the intention that workplaces must be suitable for all workers, including workers with any kind of disability.

Employees have the right to a safe and healthy workplace, which is suitable for all who work in or visit them. This means that an employer must look at issues such as space, cleanliness, lighting, ventilation, adequate toilets, washing and changing facilities.

Workplace dangers are not always obvious but paying attention to these issues and those related to areas such as emergency lighting, suitable floors, safe traffic routes, windows and doors will help to achieve this. Working practices and conditions that seem harmless can eventually lead to serious illness.

IV.II Employers' duties and those of Controllers of Premises

Employers and controllers of industrial premises have a general duty to make sure that the workplace meets certain conditions as prescribed by relevant laws and regulations. They have to pay attention to the followings:

a. *Maintenance*: make sure that the workplace, equipment, devices and systems are maintained, in working order and in good repair.

b. *Ventilation*: make sure that enclosed workplaces are well ventilated and have enough fresh and purified air.

c. *Temperature*: maintain a reasonable temperature inside building during working hours. Enough thermometers must be provided.

d. *Lighting*: must be suitable and efficient and natural as far as reasonably and practical. Emergency lighting must be provided where lighting failure would cause danger.

e. *Cleanliness*: keep workplaces and furnishings clean. Waste materials must not be allowed accumulate, except in suitable containers.

f. *Space*: make sure workrooms have enough floor area, height and unoccupied space.

g. *Workstations*: must be suitable for the worker and work. A suitable seat must be provided to employee where necessary.

h. *Floors*: must be suitable and not uneven or slippery, not presenting a safety risk. They must be kept free from obstructions likely to cause a slip, trip or fall. Handrails must be provided on staircases, except where they would obstruct traffic.

i. *Falls*: take suitable and sufficient measures to prevent people falling or being struck by falling objects. Tanks must be securely covered and fenced where there is a risk of a person falling into a dangerous substance.

j. *Windows*: make sure that windows, and transparent and translucent surfaces, consist of safe material, and are clearly marked, and safe when open.

k. *Traffic*: organise workplaces to allow safe traffic circulation by pedestrians and vehicles.

l. *Doors*: make sure that doors and gates are suitably constructed and comply with certain safety specifications.

m. *Escalators (lifts)*: make that sure escalators function safely, equipped with necessary safety devices and fitted with easily identifiable and readily accessible emergency stop controls.

n. *Toilets*: provide suitable and sufficient sanitary conveniences at readily accessible places.

o. *Washing*: provide suitable and sufficient washing facilities at readily accessible places.

p. *Water*: provide an adequate supply of wholesome drinking water and cups, readily accessible and conspicuously marked.

q. *Clothing*: provide suitable and sufficient accommodation for clothing, as well as changing facilities where special clothing is worn.

r. *Restrooms*: provide suitable and sufficient rest facilities at readily accessible places. Rest rooms and areas must include suitable arrangements to protect non-smokers from discomfort. Suitable facilities must be provided for pregnant or nursing employees to rest and for employees to eat meals.

IV.III Mandatory Duties of Employers

Under the law, employers must:

a. decide what could harm employees in their job and take precautions to stop it;

b. explain how risks will be controlled and tell employees who is responsible for health and safety;

c. give employees the training and information they need to do their job safely;

d. provide employees with any equipment and protective clothing they need and ensure it is maintained;

e. provide toilets, washing facilities and drinking water;

f. provide first aid facilities;

g. record injuries, diseases and dangerous incidents at work and report these to the Health and Safety Manager where relevant;

h.   have insurance that covers employees in case they get hurt at work or ill through work-related;

i.   work with anyone sharing the workplace or anyone who is providing employees (such as agency), so that everyone's health and safety is protected.

In the same token, employees have health and safety responsibilities as mentioned here below:

a.   follow any training they have received when using equipment or materials the employer has given them;

b.   take reasonable care of their own and other people's health and safety;

c.   co-operate with their employer on health and safety; and

d.   tell someone if you think the work or inadequate precautions are putting anyone's health and safety at risk.

How do you know what is reasonable and practicable?

The law requires employers to eliminate risks so far as is reasonable and practicable. To decide what is reasonable and practicable, one must consider the followings:

a.   the likelihood of the hazard or risk occurring;

b.   the harm that would result from the hazard or risk;

c.   what a person knows (or should know) about the hazard or risk, and what are the ways to eliminate or reduce it; and

d.   Availability and suitability of ways to eliminate or reduce the hazard or cost of eliminating or reducing the hazard or risk.

CHAPTER 5

Vicarious Liability

'Qui facit per alium facit per se' (A person who acts through other acts himself) and

'Qui sentit commodum debet sentire et onus'

(a person who takes the benefit ought also to take the burden).

Vicarious liability refers to a situation where someone is held responsible for the actions or omissions of another person. In a workplace context, an employer can be liable for the acts or omissions of its employees, provided that it can be shown that the acts or omission took place in the course of the employment.

Vicarious liability is a strict liability. This means the employer is still liable even though he or she is not at fault. There are two main types of vicarious liability. The first is employer-employee, where the employer is vicariously liable for the employee's wrongdoing committed "in the course of employment". The second kind is where the wrongdoing results in the breach of what has been described as a non-delegable duty owed by the defendant to the claimant, for example licensees owing a non-delegable duty to their clients.

A non-delegable duty usually arises out of a pre-existing relationship between the claimant and the defendant. As a result of that relationship, the defendant owes the claimant a duty to take reasonable care to see that he, or his property, is not harmed. That duty cannot be delegated. The performance of the duty may be delegated to another. But if he is negligent in performing the duty the defendant will remain personally liable for the negligence.

V.I Understanding what Vicarious Liability means for Employers

Many employers are unaware that they can be liable for a range of actions committed by their employees in the course of their employment - these can include, but not limited to bullying and harassment, violent or discriminatory acts or even libel and breach of copyright. It's also possible to take action against an employer for the behaviour of third parties, such as clients and customers, provided these parties are deemed to be under the control of the employer.

The key question of any case of vicarious liability is whether the employee was acting in a personal capacity, or in the course of their employment. This can often be difficult to determine. Nor does an employer's liability end once the employee leaves the organisation - as the law stands, action can still be taken against an employer even though the person in question no longer works for them.

So what practical steps can employers take to avoid vicarious liability for the acts of their employees? The most important thing that employers can do is to ensure that they have taken all reasonable steps to prevent such acts or omissions from occurring. For example, maintaining an up-to-date equal opportunities policy and providing anti-discrimination training to staff serve to demonstrate an active commitment on the part of the employer towards combating discriminatory practices in the workplace. This would then reduce the likelihood of an employer being held vicariously liable for any discriminatory acts committed by its employees.

V.II Vicarious Liability in Employment

Employers can be held liable for the actions or omissions during the commission of the employee's job. In order for the act to be considered to have taken place "in the course of employment," the employer must have authorized or directed the act or be otherwise connected with the act. An employer is not, however, responsible for actions taken by the employee, which are not within the scope of employment.

The nature of employment is changing, and this brings with it the need to reconsider the rules of vicarious liability as to those for whom an employer should be liable. In recent years government policy indicating the preferred nature of the employment market has brought about considerable changes in employment practices and these have been reflected in employment laws. Not only has there been a drift towards self-employment but also a rise in such categories as casual workers, agency workers and trainees, and at the same time there has been a rise in legalism in employment laws which have produced a number of technicalities specific to that subject. Undue concentration on the contract of employment and the rise of the concept of mutuality of obligation mean that we now have a view of the nature of 'employment' which is skewed towards the demands of employment laws and the policies embedded therein.

An interesting side-line relating to this point is provided by the radical dissenting judgment of La Forest J in *London Drugs v Kuehne and Nagel* (1992) 97 DLR 4th 261, which involved an action for full damages against individual employees for damaging the plaintiff's transformer when the liability of the employer was limited to $40 by an exemption clause. In holding that the employees were not liable in tort at all (although the employers were vicariously liable) La Forest J was particularly concerned with the relationship between the plaintiffs and the employers and their expectations and reliance, but although the judgment is expressly limited to the narrow problem in issue, the conclusion does suggest that where the act is being done by the enterprise and the other party has neither reliance upon nor expectations of the individuals concerned, it makes sense to say that the act is only that of the employer.

V.III Elements of Vicarious Liability of an Employer

Most often, a victim is required to demonstrate that the elements of vicarious liability exist. If he/she fails to do so, the court may find that the employer is not liable for the damages. The primary element of vicarious liability that must be proven is:

a. Whether there is an agreement that the employee has entered into as a condition of employment that required the employee to work under the authority of the employer.

b. Additional elements of vicarious liability require the employer to have control over the employee, and the actions of the employee to have fallen within the scope of employment at the time of the incident.

For instance:

Lado hires Garang as a forklift operator. While moving a large crate to the customer-loading zone, Garang hits a customer's car, damaging it. Garang was engaged in the duties required by his employment, therefore Lado can be held vicarious liable for the damages.

V.IV Scope of Employment

It is always of paramount important to tackle the issue of the scope of employment (work) as it is the core cornerstone in the establishment of vicarious liability. Scope of works refers the terms of employment (terms of reference). It varies, depending on the specific requirements of the job the employee is hired to do. There are several instances however, where a worker can be deemed to have worked outside the scope of employment.

Scope of employment refers to a person actively involved in an employment at a particular time. Also, in order to hold an employer liable for the wrongful acts of an employee, it may be necessary to show that the employee was engaged in duties in the scope of employment at the time of the wrongful conduct.

The test is whether the actions of an employee further the business of the employer and are not personal business, thereby making an employer liable for damages due to such actions under the doctrine of *"respondeat superior"*. For example, if an employee is en-route to deliver goods to a customer and makes a detour to do a personal errand, any accident occurring while on the personal errand are not in the scope of employment and the employer is thus not liable. It is also referred to as *"course of employment"*.

For instance:

An Independent Contractor – any individual performing work for someone else, though not considered legally as employee, but independent contractor, do perform his/her work outside the scope of employment only in relation to vicarious liability.

Illegal Acts – the commission of an illegal act is not within the scope of employment. Any damages caused by the illegal act, or during the commission of the illegal act, are not considered an employer's responsibility in most cases.

V.V Employee Acting Outside Scope of Employment

Employers whose employee engages in an activity that was not directed or controlled by the employer may not be directly responsible for damages.

This depends on what the activity was, and what purpose it served. For instance, an employee simply taking a "detour" while in the business of his/her employer, such as stopping to get gas while making deliveries, may still expose the employer to liability. Having gas in the vehicle is necessary to making the employer's deliveries.

However, on the other hand, an employee who remembers her child forgot her permission slip to the school activity and thus runs home to pick it up, then delivers it to the school, while he/she is supposed to be making those deliveries, is definitely not engaged in the employer's business. Any damages caused during such detour, say from having a traffic accident while rushing to the school, is not the employer's responsibility. This is known as an employee "frolic act."

V.VI Vicarious Liability in Medical Care

In a medical setting, a hospital or doctor can be held vicariously liable for a claim based on the acts of one of its employees. This includes the actions of its physicians, nurses, laboratory personnel, other technicians, administrative employees, and other staff members.

In order to avoid the possibility of vicarious liability, hospitals, clinics, and doctors ensure that all of their employees have the necessary qualifications and credentials needed to perform their jobs. If a physician or other healthcare provider is considered an independent contractor of a hospital, vicarious liability may not apply, though laws and legal interpretation on this vary and thus beg clarity.

Example of Vicarious Liability in Medical Care

Latjor experienced an abdominal pain that felt as if he has a broken rib, few weeks after he had abdominal surgery at the local hospital. He went to the Emergency Department of the same hospital for x-ray. The x-ray showed that a surgical clamp had been left inside Latjor's abdominal cavity, which required immediate surgery for removal. Latjor can opt to sue the surgeon for medical malpractice and negligent, but he can also sue the hospital, on the ground of vicarious liability for the actions of its physicians.

V.VII Other Types of Vicarious Liability

Vicarious liability may apply to a number of situations in which someone other than the person who caused damages has some type of control, direction, or ownership in the situation. The most common other types of vicarious liability include principal liability and parental liability.

Principal Liability

An automobile owner can be held vicariously liable if he lends his vehicle to another person and that person causes damage or injury through negligence or reckless driving. This applies mostly in the cases where the driver was using the car in order to perform a task for the owner of the vehicle.

Example of Principal Liability

Habakkuk, who recently had surgery on his broken leg, lends his car to Akello so that she can run personal errands for him. As Akello is pulling out of the parking lot at Habakkuk's bank, she hits another vehicle. Habakkuk may be held vicariously liable for Akello accident.

If, on the other hand, Akello kept Habakkuk's car for use while he is laying in his sickbed, and she hit another car while driving to the grocery store, for her own needs, Habakkuk is likely not to be held vicariously liable. Simply lending a car to someone does not expose the owner to liability for the driver's actions. The driver would need to be acting in the service of the owner.

Parental Liability

There is a serious debate in the legal fraternity on the parental liability. Some legal scholars on one hand argued that parents could be held directly liable for their children acts as if it is their own actions. This should be the case if the parents allowed a child to drive, or parents leave a loaded gun within a place reachable by a child. If the child in either circumstance caused harm by taking advantage of the opportunity left before him/her by the parents, the parents can be held directly liable.

Other legal scholars hold a view that, parents may be held vicariously liable for negligent acts committed by their child, only when the parents failed to provide adequate supervision. This is the view held in South Sudan Customary Legal practice and it is the question whether this view will gain legal recognition and thus become the legal doctrine.

Example of Parental Liability

Napon works eight hours a day and cannot afford to hire a babysitter to watch her ten (10) and twelve (12) years old boys after school. She feels they are old enough to take care of themselves during that short time until she gets home. One afternoon, Napon's sons joined other neighbourhood children in throwing rocks at a neighbour's backyard workshop, breaking out three windows. In this situation, Napon may be held vicariously or direct liable for her sons' destructive acts and be ordered to repair the neighbour's windows.

Court Ruling in Partrick Lynch vs Cavan Town Cattle Market

Patrick Lynch was a cattle drover for the Cavan Town Cattle Market. In 2010, he and two other employees were supposed to be herding cattle between pens, on the way to the auction floor. This is a three men job, but Patrick's fellow employees left to take care of their own business, leaving him to move the cattle by himself. While moving through the pens to open a gate, Patrick had to pass behind a large bull, which kicked him in the groin, causing serious injuries. Patrick filed a civil lawsuit against Cavan Town Cattle Market, claiming his injuries were a direct result of his employer's negligence. The employer responded, stating that the employee should not have performed the duties if the job was unreasonably risky. The court ruled in favour of the employer and argued had it not been negligent and overlooking negligence on the part of the other two employees, the situation would have been prevented.

V.VIII The Vicarious Liability of Employers – Worth another Look[25]

Given the recent media attention on the conduct of employees in New Zealand workplaces, it is worthwhile to have a fresh look at the law on the vicarious liability of employers for the actions of their employees.

It has long been the case that, at common law, an employer is vicariously liable for the tortious acts of its employees, if the acts are carried out in the course of employment and bear a sufficient connection to the employee's role. The recent application of this test in the United Kingdom has demonstrated that it may be difficult for employers to avoid vicarious liability

---

[25] LAWTALK 917, Maria Dew and Anjori Mitra, May 2018.

claims, even where the employer would never have sanctioned the employee's conduct. This raises the question of how that test might be applied in New Zealand and worldwide labour market.

The "close connection" test

The close connection test was originally formulated in the leading English text, Salmond and Heuston on the Law of Torts, and developed in two key cases: the decision of the Supreme Court of Canada in *Bazley v Curry [1999] 2 SCR 534* and of the House of Lords, United Kingdom in *Lister v Hesley Hall Ltd [2002] 1 AC 215*. The facts of those cases are similar. In both cases, the defendant operated a residential care facility for children and was held to be vicariously liable for sexual abuse by an employee. Those cases confirmed the approach to vicarious liability was as follows:

[First, the existence of a relationship of employment between the wrongdoer and the party alleged to be vicariously liable, or a relationship akin to employment (e.g. an agency relationship).

Secondly, a sufficient connection between the wrongful act and the scope of the wrongdoer's role as employee or agent. This involves consideration of the scope of the wrongdoer's role and the relationship between that role and the wrongful act.]

At first glance, it seems an employer should never be held liable for criminal acts of sexual abuse, given most employers would never authorise such acts. However, the court in both *Bazley v Curry* and *Lister v Hesley Hall Ltd* held that because the relevant employee had been given extensive supervisory duties over young children, with little oversight by others, the circumstances met the "close connection" test. The environment in which the abuse occurred was connected to the employment and vicarious liability was imposed. Vicarious liability for sexual abuse was also imposed on employers in similar circumstances in *Maga v Archbishop of Birmingham [2010] WLR 1441 (CA)* and *Various Claimants v Catholic Child Welfare Society [2013] 2 AC.*

In 2016, the United Kingdom courts further considered the "close connection" test. In *Cox v Ministry of Justice [2016] AC 664*, the UK Supreme Court held the Ministry of Justice was vicariously liable for injuries caused by a prisoner negligently dropping a heavy bag of rice on another prisoner. Both prisoners had been assigned to work in the kitchen by the Ministry (although they were not technically employed by the Ministry).

Another decision of the UK Supreme Court from 2016 was *Mohamud v Wm Morrison Supermarkets plc [2016] AC 677*. Here, the employee was a sales attendant at a petrol station. The claimant stopped at the petrol station and, after requesting assistance, was subjected to racist and abusive language from the employee. The employee then followed the claimant as he walked back to his car and subjected him to a serious physical assault.

The Supreme Court, on appeal, held the employer was vicariously liable for the employee's torts of assault and battery. The court confirmed the established test was to inquire as to the nature of the employee's job and then to ask whether there was sufficient connection between that job and the employee's wrongful conduct to make it right as a matter of social justice, for the employer to be held liable. The court acknowledged that this required an evaluative judgment in each case having regard to the circumstances. The court held in this case the employee's role was to interact with customers, the assault was on the employer's premises, he was on duty and the interaction was therefore within the "field of activities" that had been assigned to the employee – even though the assault was never sanctioned by the employer. There was sufficient connection between the role and the wrongful conduct to hold the employer vicariously liable.

By contrast, another 2016 case, *Bellman v Northampton Recruitment Ltd [2016] EWHC 3104 (QB)*, dismissed the claim of vicarious liability against the employer. The employer's Managing Director had committed an assault on a Sales Manager after the employer's Christmas party. The court held the assault was not sufficiently connected to the Managing Director's employment, as it occurred during "an entirely independent, voluntary, and discreet early hour drinking session of a very different nature to the Christmas party and unconnected with the defendant's business".

CHAPTER SIX

Unions and Industrial Relations

Unions are organizations that negotiate with corporations, businesses and other organizations on behalf of union members. There are trade unions, which represent workers who do a particular type of job, and industrial unions, which represent workers in a particular industry.

Trade unions, also known as labour unions, have been an important part of the market labour movement since eighteenth (18th) centaury. The relationship between labour unions and employers has often been contentious, but the truth is that labour unions play an important role in the way employers and employees function together to create a harmonious workplace.

Unions are important because they help set the standards for education, skill levels, wages, working conditions, and quality of life for workers. Union-negotiated wages and benefits are generally superior to what non-union workers receive. Most union contracts provide far more protections than nation-states laws.

Employers and workers seem to approach employment from vastly different perspectives. So how can the two sides reach an agreement? The answer lies in unions. Unions have played a role in the worker-employer dialogue for centuries, but in the last few decades, many aspects of the business environment have changed. With this in mind, it's important to understand how unions fit into the current business environment, and what role unions play in the modern economy.

VI.I The Role of Trade Unions in Industrial Relations

One of the most important roles that labour unions play is that when there is a dispute in the workplace, the union acts as an intermediary between employees and business owners. Labour union leaders are experienced at solving problems through formal arbitration and grievance procedures. Instead of viewing this process as contentious, business owners should welcome the involvement of a union representative, because it can expedite the resolution. When issues arise at the workplace between employer and employee, the goal is to secure a "win-win" in which both sides feel as if they each attained something from the deal.

VI.II Save Employer Time Through Collective Bargaining

Every labour union operates under what is known as the collective bargaining agreement, which helps secure fair wages, working hours, benefits, and the standards necessary for wage increment. The collective bargaining agreement also protects employees from being fired without just cause, which protects employer from litigation, because employer can only terminate a worker if that worker violated company's standards and policies. Some employers view the collective bargaining agreement as a necessary evil, but employers should view it as a way to save company the time and money of having to negotiate wages, wage increment and benefits.

VI.III Help Reduce Turnover Rate

The goal of most labour unions is not to create conflict with businesses; however, the goal is to ensure that employees are treated fairly, and that they feel comfortable and secure on the job. When that goal is achieved, employees tend to stick around, instead of trying to find a more favourable situation. Union members earn an estimated thirty (30%) percent more in wages than do non-unionized workers, and ninety-two (92%) percent of unionized workers have health insurance, compared to non-unionized workers. Another union benefit is that union workers are much more likely to secure guaranteed pensions than non-unionized workers. By ensuring fair wages and benefits, labour unions help keep the membership content, and workers who are satisfied with their jobs are more likely to work hard, instead of looking for a quick way to exit their job.

VI.IV Objectives of Industrial Relations and why Industrial Relations are Important

The important and objectives of industrial relations are to facilitate production; to safeguard the rights and interests of both labour and management by enlisting the cooperation of both; to achieve a sound, harmonious and mutual beneficial relationship between employers and employees.

a. Continuity of Production

The most vital function of industrial relations is ensuring of an uninterrupted production. This means that all positions of employment, from managers to workers, are always filled so that full-scale production is maximized. In fact, the industries rely on one another. Therefore, the logical goals of industrial relations, is to ensure that there is never a breakdown in communication or degradation of an industrial relationship leading to a stall in productivity and thus a stall in economic gain. This leads us to the second reason as to why the good industrial relations are vital.

b. Minimize the occurrence of Industrial Disputes

Good industrial relations aim to minimize, if not eradicate, the occurrence of strikes, sit-in, lockouts and grievances, which hampers industrial activities.

c. Minimize Wastage

Good industrial relations help increase and ensure continuous production. It thus helps minimize wastage of labour and material resources.

VI.V How do Industrial Relations Benefit the Employee?

Union Representatives: Trade and/or labour unions resist the exploitation of employees by employers through equal bargaining power and represent workers' interests in the employment relationship. It is the union (rep), on behalf of the worker, who ensures that the employee benefits from Industrial Relations and aim to secure the workers by helping them to have:

a. Better wages that is sustainable for the future of the employee.

b. Improved working conditions so that the employee can be productive, safe and happy.

c. Mutual respect by on-going conversation between the employer and employees to keep the work relationship healthy.

d. The proper training and skills development to keep up with trends in the workplace so the employee will be able to progress within their career.

Labour Union also ensure that the process of Industrial Relations benefits the employee and protects the interests of the employee during negotiations and similar relations with the employer.

VI.VI How does Unions benefit employees from Industrial Relations?

Ever heard the saying *"there's strength in numbers"*?

Collective Bargaining: Labour unions represent the interests of a body of employees by means of a united front. This allows the employees' voices to be heard more effectively than if employees made the same requests or voiced the same concerns one by one in their individual capacity.

Unions have the power to organize strikes, boycotts, sit-ins and formal protests in order to get the employers' attention and urge them to consider matters from the perspective of the employees that the trade unions represent.

Employee Welfare: Unions look out for the best interests of their members. Unionized workers, for instance, earn higher wages than their non-unionized counterparts, and they automatically have an intermediary who will step in for them during negotiations with employers about work schedules, income, safety etc.

Unions also exist in order to protect employees' basic rights such as the right to access healthcare and be protected from accident and injury in the workplace.

VI.VII The Role of Government in Industrial Relations

The government and its agencies through the government's construction, passing and implementation of relevant industrial relations law, policies and regulations etc., influence the processes of industrial relations and the relationships between employees and employers.

The government and/or its agencies, possibly in consultation with stakeholders in the industrial relations processes, determine the legal framework within which Industrial Relations must function. The legal framework can be the legal limitations imposed on an employer/employee relationship.

For instance: the number of hours an employee is allowed to legally work per week and how much an employer is obligated to pay an employee for a certain amount of work.

In South Africa, for example, the BCEA (Basic Conditions of Employment Act) can be seen as a governmental contribution to the governing of the relationship between employers and employees and can as such be considered the government's contribution to guiding the processes of industrial relations.

Judge and jury:

The government can also become directly or indirectly involved in the industrial relations processes as mediator when boundaries are overstepped, or negotiations go awry.

The government could become involved in, for example, settling an industrial relations dispute in court, or adjusting or amending a policy which has proven itself flawed, out-dated or newly irrelevant following the outcome of a certain case or set of negotiations.

How does the government benefit from Industrial Relations?

Basically, the government benefits from Industrial Relations in a way: a safe working environment promotes employee and employer satisfaction, which in turn helps maintain high employment rates which reflects well on the government and directly addresses and influences issues such as poverty and crime.

VI.VIII Industrial Relations in Society and what Role does it play

The society benefits from Industrial Relations by achieving the following objectives:

Wages and living standard: Industrial Relations forms part of the process to ensure that each and every employed individual in our country is making a wage that improves his/her living standard. The minimum wage policy should be of concern to every person in our society.

Not only the poor and/or unskilled benefit from wages – so do all industries and enterprises at large. If all our manual labourers earn a wage, they will have more capital to cater to their basic needs and wants. This will essentially ensure that people have enough money to spend in order to satisfy their basic needs and that benefits everybody, albeit indirectly at times, because it means more money plugged back into our economy.

Equal opportunity: Industrial Relations processes aim to achieve an equal opportunity within our country's workplaces. Anybody who is not able-bodied male / female stands to benefit from strides taken toward equal opportunity.

Those who campaigns, through Industrial Relations channels, for equal opportunity are campaigning for equal treatment and opportunity in the workplace free from the effects of preference or prejudice and unhampered by any tribal or social class barriers.

Rights of the individual: what is the definition of individual rights? Imagine a world where you could not own property or a right to protect yourself and your family. You could not vote for the candidate of your choice in elections, could not speak freely without being arrested, and could not practice the religion you wanted. Imagine you could have your house searched by law enforcement at any time without a search warrant or be subjected to cruel and unusual punishment for committing a crime. Imagine you being subjected to a work you do not want to do.

In such a world, you would have no individual rights. The Republic of South Sudan was established based on democratic principles, and individual rights coincide with democracy. Democracy can be defined at the lens of individual rights, as everyone in society having formal equality of rights and privileges. The people's representatives put these ideals of democracy in the Constitution in 2011, and they continue to exist to this day.

Your individual rights guarantee individuals' rights to certain freedoms without interference from the government or other individuals. These rights are derived from the Bill of Rights in the Constitution. The Bill of Rights consists of the first ten amendments of the Constitution. Within the Bill of Rights, your individual rights are specified. They apply to everyone within South Sudan borders. Such rights are also protected in the Industrial Relations.

Hence, there are processes and mechanisms in place in sphere of Industrial Relations that are in place to help protect the rights of the individual. This means that, even if you are not currently employed, the Industrial Relations processes are campaigning on your behalf, already fighting for your rights to be respected, should you ever enter an industry.

Work and life balance: A balance between work and your personal life is extremely important to keep yourself up to high standards. Industrial relations aim specifically to create a balance between being highly productive and enjoy the job you are in to the maximum.

This is beneficial to both the employee and employer in the long term. When every business/employee relationship is balanced optimally, it would have good consequences for the society at large.

VI.IX Legal ground in South Sudan Labour Act, 2017

The purpose of Labour Act, 2017 is to establish a legal framework for the minimum conditions of employment, labour relations, labour institutions, labour disputes management and provision of health and safety at the workplace. As such Collective Agreement, which is the result of collective bargaining, is defined as a written agreement concerning terms and conditions of work or any other matter of mutual interest in industrial relations concluded by one or more registered trade unions with their respective employers.

Section 89 of Labour Act, 2017 prescribed that "parties to the negotiations of a collective agreement shall negotiate in a good faith and make every effort to conclude a collective agreement". The duty to negotiate in good faith includes but not limited to:

a. attending and participating in meetings at working hours;

b. disclosing relevant information at the right time;

c. responding to proposals made by other parties to the

negotiation at the right time;

d. giving acceptable consideration to the proposals of other parties to the negotiations;

e. refraining from unfair conduct that undermines freedom of association or collective bargaining; and

f. recognizing and bargaining with the other parties to the negotiation of the collective agreement.

If any party refuses to participate in negotiation of a collective agreement, the affected party may apply to the Labour Commission for an order directing the other party to negotiate in good faith.

CONCLUSION

Absolutely everybody should know the; who, what, when, where, and why of labour relations and how industrial relations management works.

Knowledge is power, and the above should have adequately equipped you to identify and address breakdowns in communication and the subsequent halt in production or lapse in productivity.

Whether you are an employee, an employer or a casual observer, it is important that you know whom to contact in the event of a breakdown in communication or unfair treatment in the workplace. Open lines of communication are vital to on-going economic and industrial growth.

We hope this book will help to navigate you through the murky waters of industrial relations and help you understand exactly whom you have got in your corner, and who to contact in a time of industrial crisis.

Industrial relations exist to serve and protect everybody involved – from the employee, to the employer, to the public at large and all the way through to the government. If the lines of communication are open and industrial relations are undertaken, everybody wins.

ABOUT THE AUTHOR

John Kon Kelei is a law practitioner, an Advocate and Commissioner for Oath, lecturer of Law at School of Law, University of Juba. He is also an executive general manager at South Sudan Pensions Fund.

BP

Bor Publishers

www.borpublishers.com
admin@borpublishers.com